The Human Condition

Megan Whitelaw

BookLeaf Publishing

India | USA | UK

Presentation by *BookLeaf Publishing*

Web: www.bookleafpub.com

E-mail: info@bookleafpub.com

ISBN: 978-93-5744-963-2

First edition 2022

DEDICATION

This work is dedicated to my sister who encouraged me in all manner of things and examined my flaws and ill-judged activities without censure.

I know if she could read this she would be nothing but jubilant, ignoring the errors and celebrating the completion.

ACKNOWLEDGEMENT

This has been a largely secret activity. To the one that knew about the secret from the beginning, thanks for all the writing practise.

.

PREFACE

This book is the result of a challenge to myself. Write more, I would say to myself daily while doing anything but write.

I am a realist, perhaps even a 'grittest'. These poems represent slices of life, thoughts, emotions, experiences and events. Some of them are my secrets, now unveiled in public...secretly.

It's a unique feeling to know that these life snippets are out in the universe. Maybe someone will read one of these poems and have a moment of recognition, or dislike or disdain. If one person reads, stops and looks to the sky as they ponder the words, I'll be happy with that.

Indiscretion

Paramour, paramour, delicious word
Let it roll and rest in my mouth
While I run and drive, walk and work
It feels like I imagine you would

Sex and words, it's enough, you say
No mathematics with squares and points
My rounded cleavage, a stifled breath
Your gaze, your hand, a mess

Me and my shame in the cold devil's hour
Undoing and showing
While you sip your summery
Breakfast time tea

An indecent thrill, my springtime obsession
Your voice in my mind, words on my screen
Let's write a story so wicked it takes us
Plunging and rolling, wet fingered

Goodbye

Maybe it's not such a big thing
You say of your death
I look down at the fringes
Of my dance skirt
While you twist the plastic tentacles
Adorning your arm

The next time I see you
Is the last we shall speak
Your soft hand, small like mine
Reaches out to touch my cheek

Your terrified eyes at the end
Are my burden
Staying and keeping my promise was hard
I'm older than you now

Some of the young ones don't know you
Or don't remember
I was offered your treasured Christmas
decorations
But I left them behind in a white plastic bag

Too hard to admit that you'd gone

Istanbul

Istanbul

I lay on top of the tasselled bed
Listen to the men talking below
On the street
Surely smoking
And chatting
I hear the cats
Calling each other
The hum of a different city
I know I'm somewhere different

Breakfast on the terrace
Soft, soft colours
Buildings faltering under time
How can I tell you about the sea?
That flat Bosphorus
So busy with its ferries
Laden with music and
Serious, out-of-doors faces

Silver

Sometimes I wear three men

On my body

My ears, my fingers

A secret joy

When I think about each one

A gift that wasn't a gift

Reminds me of the forbidden

Long ago remnant of snowy Greece

Its flat face with garnet beam, and

A shining emblem of sensible

Like a tag

Human Condition

Fuggy suburban kitchen
Crusty, curling edges on the plates
Do-gooding lips around teacups
"F'Ghanistarrn" says the priest
Almost spitting
Pie crumbs stuck on his fat, purple lips
"All around, the human condition, you really
should see it"
"They treat dogs better here" says the dark eyed
boy next to me
Quietly

Mispent Youth

Thighs stuck to the vinyl
Holden Premier seats
The others murmuring around me
Where to go, what to do
Maybe the beach

"Come on Eileen"
Winfield Blue blistering my fingers
I'll remember this moment forever
For no reason, just to remember
Even though it wasn't important

Obsession

If obsession is secret, isn't it better?
Like a burn, a smoky smoulder
Underneath the normal
Wherever I go my obsession goes too
Making me sick with overthinking
Imagining, planning and wistful dreaming
Over time my obsession, it wanes
I chase it, checking, is it still there?
Or has it become a shame, a stupidity
A waste of my time

Stupid Nights

Pissed again
Offer me some comfort
Play my music, not yours
Hours spin quickly
We argue and dance
I'm not a good drunk
I get jealous
I snarl and attack
Take shelter
Tomorrow I'll be sweet
And cook for you

Garson

His neat body under the black apron
Square against his abdomen
Elegant hand serving, placing
I'm aware of him behind me
Hovering
Outside, leaning on the tiled wall
Sure enough, he comes
Faces together, unfamiliar kiss
Come and meet me, I whisper
I can't get away, he says
Hot against my neck
So he becomes the kiss with the waiter
Instead of anything else

The Last Night

All the words of that night are jumbled now
I love you, I hate you
I'm going
Goodbye

Waiting in nothingness
I refused to believe, yet I knew

I stepped in to the dawn light
Quiet and eerie
The car was the place you were waiting
For me
But you weren't there and I'm searching
The woodshed, not thinking
There there you are, standing
By your favourite tree

Warm and relieved I reached out to you
Speaking
My love and my greeting
Come back in the warm

You couldn't speak to me
Standing, yet legs bent
All useless and crazy

Not right

I hold you
And shake you
I'm trying to bring you
Back to me,
Make it alright

You're gone and I'm
Screaming
I'm still not believing
And nothing can make it alright

Amazon

A feeling like fire
It is hard to describe it
A power, it bursts through my chest

I walk taller
Step firmer
Glare harder
If you cross me
I'll kill you
Maybe I just need a sleep

Trauma

The day that you told me
I leant over you
To talk about your rights
Those that were stolen
And your tears slowly crept down your cheeks

Switchers

Push me and squeeze me
Force me and please me
I'll bite you and kiss you
Nip you and pinch you
Play with me, go on
Into the night

Typing...

My favourite correspondent
Ribald, removed and always ready
Don't let the moon and star
Deceive you
He's seriously irreverent and
Cares not for the phonies

Wordy like a rapper
But he doesn't believe it
Cunning as a cat
Will always amuse me
Slow to move and hot to touch

Distance

If you find me, don't hail me
Just watch me go by
Don't break the spell
Let's stay other-worldly
A schema, a vision
Imaginary only

Power Imbalance

So studiously he stirs
A tiny wooden stick
In a pregnant tea glass
The downward glance of the introvert
I stare at the crimson drops on the saucer
Grasping for something to charm and assuage
The word for cheese, I say
I've just forgotten it
A smile then, shoulders back
He'll be my hero today

F#%@ER

As we walk by that old hotel
His face lobs out of the window
Sodden and bloated
In a sharky drawl he tells me
What he'd like to do with me
What parts he'd like to touch
Rage, rage, rage
Unfurled at him
Blasting him
He's shocked I don't want him
What I want is a gun

Identity

Which one am I?
The sturdy mother, steering the ship
The interested friend
The surly wife
What about that blousy, wanton
brassy whore?
The smarty-pants reader
With glasses and bookshelves
The all-giving therapist
The rage-filled recounter
When you find out the answer
Tell me
I have no bloody idea

I'm Hiding

You've got many secrets, he said
It's probably true
Secrets in my mind, what I'll share and what I
won't
Boxes and notebooks
Computer files
All with secrets
When I die don't look at them
Throw them away
Or make a big bonfire
And think of me while you watch the flames
The old me without the secrets